How to be More in Tune with The Feelings of Your Customers

Using Emotional Intelligence to Increase Sales, Customer Loyalty and Retention

Sam Amoo

For Questions and enquiries contact;

sam@samamoo.com

ISBN: 978-1-63750-356-0

Sam Amoo Publishing

Special Bonus

Other Books

- Sell Like Titans
- Time Management For Busy People

Table of Contents

HOW TO BE MORE IN TUNE WITH THE FEELINGS OF YOUR CUSTOMERS **1**

S P E C I A L B O N U S **4**

O T H E R B O O K S **5**

INTRODUCTION **8**

CHAPTER 1 ..... **16**

WHAT IS EMOTIONAL INTELLIGENCE? 16

How to Identify the Emotional Needs of Your Customer, and How to Meet Them *23*

Why is Emotional Intelligence Important? *30*

How to Develop Emotional Intelligence Skills? *33*

Deliberate Practice of Emotional Intelligence *39*

CHAPTER 2 ..... **43**

HOW TO IDENTIFY YOUR CUSTOMER'S EMOTIONAL STYLE 43

Engaging Your Customers with the Right Message at the Right Time *52*

How to Increase Customer Loyalty *57*

How To Increase Customer Retention *59*

The Art of Empathy and its Effect on Customer Loyalty *62*

How to Build Rapport with Customers *65*

Knowing and Understanding the Customer's Personality Traits *68*

Understanding Personality Types *70*

How You Can Best Cater Your Brand to Suit the Unique Needs of Your Customers *72*

Recognizing and Appreciating the Different Needs of Customers *73*

Knowing Your Customers' Motivations *76*

Building Customer Relationships *78*

Creating a Loyal Client Base *79*

CHAPTER 3 ..... **82**

UNDERSTANDING YOUR CUSTOMERS' EMOTIONS 82

Why You Should Listen to the Feeling Inside Your Customer's Head *84*

Understanding the Dynamics of Human Emotions *87*

Recognizing the Differences Between Emotions and Feelings *90*

How to Interpret Your Customer's Feelings ... *95*

CHAPTER 4 ... **99**

Rules to Creating Great Product and How to Keep Customers ... 99

Improving Your Relationship Management Skills and Building a Customer Advisory Board ... *108*

CHAPTER 5 ... **117**

Importance of Maintaining an Ethical Environment in the Workplace ... 117

Helping Your Employees Overcome Feelings of Anxiety and Low Self-esteem in the Business Space ... *120*

Establishing a Reliable Reputation and Track Record ... *122*

CHAPTER 6 ... **127**

Applying Emotional Intelligence to Marketing Strategies ... 127

How to Use Emotions to Increase Sales and Retention ... *129*

CHAPTER 7 ... **135**

Developing a Winning Culture in Business ... 135

How to Encourage Customers to Refer ... *137*

Conclusion ... 139

SPECIAL BONUS ... **142**

THANK YOU! ... **143**

ABOUT THE AUTHOR ... **145**

O T H E R B O O K ... **146**

Introduction

If you're looking to increase sales, customer loyalty and retention then you need to learn how to be in tune with the feelings of your customers. If you want to increase your customer loyalty, you'll need to understand the emotions that are driving their buying decisions. That's why this book will help you learn how to be more in tune with the feelings of your customers—and how to use emotional intelligence to increase customer loyalty and retention.

Emotions are a key element of sales, brand loyalty and customer retention. They affect the buying decisions of your customers, and therefore they should be considered a primary marketing tool. By tapping into the subconscious part of their brain, entrepreneurs can increase customer loyalty and retention by getting better at understanding customer emotions. If you're like most small business owners, customer retention is a big part of your marketing strategy.

So, <u>how do you know if you're doing enough to ensure that customers feel valued and satisfied? And how do you find out what those feelings are so you can effectively target them?</u>

The secret is to use an emotion-based approach to marketing.

Emotions are a form of communication that everyone understands. They're not complicated, and yet they have the power to shape human behavior. In fact, it's estimated that more than 90% of all customer interactions begin with an emotional response.

So; why not take advantage of the latest advances in emotional intelligence research, and use it to increase your chances of keeping your current customers and attracting new ones?

What is emotional intelligence?

Emotional intelligence is a concept that was developed by **Daniel Goleman** in his book **"Emotional Intelligence"**. *Goleman* defined emotional intelligence as *"the ability to perceive, assimilate, express and regulate emotions, and to understand and motivate oneself through emotion."* Goleman believes that people with high emotional intelligence are better able to manage their own feelings and emotions, while also understanding others and managing relationships. He also suggests that emotional intelligence is a more important predictor of success than **IQ**.

It is the ability to feel empathy and understand oneself and others. If you are able to be empathetic toward your customers and see them as human beings, you can be in tune with their feelings. It's a set of skills that can be developed through personal and professional development.

In business, emotional intelligence is the ability to identify your own emotions and those of others, understand how they impact decision-making, understand your own and others' needs and desires, and also to know how to influence others. Emotional intelligence is critical for leadership. The ability to understand and control your emotions will help you to make better decisions and lead your team with more effectiveness.

As a leader, you must be aware of your own emotions so that you can understand how you affect others. You should recognize when you are feeling angry, sad, frustrated, anxious or other negative feelings. Your emotional state will impact your communication style, your ability to motivate others, and your relationships with colleagues. To gain emotional intelligence, you must first become aware of your emotions. To do this, you must understand your personal emotional strengths and weaknesses. Knowing your strengths will help you to identify and understand your emotions more clearly.

Here are some questions to help you determine how well you're emotionally intelligent:

- Do you tend to take other people's feelings into account when making decisions?
- Do you know how to read people's body language and facial expressions?
- Can you recognize what you feel and how it affects you?
- Do you understand how to communicate with others in a way that is most likely to lead to success?

A recent study found that nearly half of consumers say they feel like the marketing messages being sent to them are often contradictory. They want to know that the products they buy are safe and healthy, but at the same time, they are drawn to products that are socially responsible. As a result, more than half of consumers shopping at a mall will prefer to buy products from companies that are socially responsible or environmentally friendly.

In addition, the more sustainable the product, the better. However, on the flip side, consumers may be aware of a good product but are unwilling to buy it or try it out because of the false representation of the product, brand owner, or social irresponsibility.

When you think about a product, it's almost inevitable that you think about the features and benefits it provides. However, what you might not realize is that the way that you think about your product can also affect its success and overall marketability. When people are dissatisfied with the service or product they're getting, they are more likely to look elsewhere for better service or a better product.

The most successful e-commerce stores rely on emotion to sell products, rather than simply listing a bunch of products and hoping people will buy something. *They know how to turn passion into profits and build customer loyalty, using proven psychological principles.*

As an entrepreneur, it's important to keep your customers happy. Customers who feel valued are more likely to come back, refer friends, and tell their networks about your business. And as you may already know, customers with higher levels of trust and satisfaction are less likely to shop elsewhere. But with a wide variety of products and services available, it's difficult to know which ones to offer, and how to differentiate your brand and business.

So; if you're looking to increase sales, customer retention and loyalty, one tactic to consider is building an emotional relationship with your customers.

Today's customer wants to be part of the buying experience. They want to feel connected to the brand.

They don't want to feel like a number. But they also don't want to be bombarded with endless emails, phone calls, and letters.

So; *how do you connect with the emotions of your customers?*

If you have a product that solves a problem for your customers, you're going to be able to increase sales, your customer loyalty, and retention—and ultimately, your profit margins—by delivering better products, faster than your competitors. You can also use the science of customer emotions to improve customer satisfaction. But in addition to increasing your customer satisfaction, you can also use this knowledge to increase your customer's loyalty and trust in your company, by creating products that are emotionally connected with your customers. You need to know what type of customers you are dealing with, and what they are hoping to accomplish when visiting your store.

This book will give you insight into how emotional intelligence affects sales, customer loyalty and retention.

- You'll learn about the different ways emotional intelligence impacts your customers.
- How to spot and manage emotions in others, and the benefits of emotional intelligence when dealing with customers.
- Understand what emotional intelligence is and how it applies to customer loyalty and retention.
- Identify the different ways emotional intelligence impacts your customers.
- Determine which emotions are driving your customers' decisions and actions.
- Learn to build great products and services.
- Gain insight into why emotional intelligence is beneficial for improving customer loyalty and retention.

...and more!

Most businesses lack emotional intelligence because they focus too much on rational thinking. As a result, they miss out on the human connections that can bring them success. The key to emotional intelligence is learning how to control your emotions. This will help you become a better leader and improve your relationships. You'll need to practice emotional self-awareness. This involves being able to recognize what you're feeling and why you feel that way. It also means having the ability to control your emotions and manage your reactions.

This book has been written as a guide for businesses looking to build loyalty amongst their customers, whether it be through improving their products and services or increasing sales.

Chapter 1

What is Emotional Intelligence?

Emotional intelligence (EI) is simply the ability to perceive, control, and understand emotions. It's considered a skill that enables us to cope with the emotional demands of everyday life. **EI** is also considered an essential talent needed for success. People with high **EI** tend to score higher on tests of intelligence, and are more effective leaders than people with low **EI**.

An important part of marketing today is to understand and harness your customers' emotions. If you're not using emotion to guide your marketing efforts, then it may be time to consider how you can better use this powerful force in your marketing strategy.

Understanding the emotional drivers behind customer behavior is key to developing successful marketing strategies

---

Understanding the emotional drivers behind customer behavior is key to developing successful marketing strategies. In fact, it's one of the three pillars of psychology that every marketer should know about (the other two being motivation and attention).

Emotion is a powerful driver of human behavior. And it's especially important when it comes to marketing. As the **Harvard Business Review** puts it,

> *"The best way to get people to buy what you are selling is to get inside their heads and understand their emotions."*

But what exactly is emotion?

Emotions are thoughts, feelings, and sensations that occur in response to an object, event, or situation. Emotions are biological reactions to stimuli that happen in real time. They are natural and involuntary. For example, you may feel happy when your child gets good grades or angry when your spouse breaks a promise. Emotions drive our behavior and influence our decision making. They can motivate us to act in a certain way. When we're feeling negative emotions, we tend to avoid things or people.

When we're feeling positive emotions, we tend to approach things or people. The emotions we experience while interacting with other people are called social emotions, and they include liking someone, disliking someone, wanting to know more about someone, and feeling bad about someone. Social emotions help us understand how others feel about us and make decisions about whether to like or dislike them. They also help us develop relationships by letting us know what people think about us.

Social emotions don't just influence our behavior; they also influence our thinking. They can change the way you think about someone or something. For example, if you find out that your friend likes you, you may feel good about yourself. In contrast, if you find out that your friend dislikes you, you may think less of yourself. Similarly, when you think about a person or an idea, you may have feelings of liking or disliking for them.

In addition, social emotions influence how you think about yourself. If you feel bad about yourself, you may not like yourself very much. On the other hand, if you feel good about yourself, you may like yourself more. When we are young, we tend to think that everyone has the same feelings as we do. However, as we grow older, we realize that people don't always share our feelings. In fact, they often have different feelings than us.

So, *why do people have different feelings?*

The answer to this question is that each person has their own unique combination of genes. Each person also has a unique experience in life.

EI is the ability to understand your own emotions, recognize others' emotions, and manage your own and other people's emotions. People with high emotional intelligence have better relationships, tend to have more satisfying lives, and achieve more professionally. And emotional intelligence is something we can develop and learn. There are different schools of thought around how to teach emotional intelligence. Most agree that teaching emotional intelligence isn't the same thing as teaching a person to be emotionally intelligent. It's just like learning a new language. You don't learn to speak the language without practice and exposure. The same applies to emotional intelligence. The best teachers for emotional intelligence are those who have practiced it themselves.

Emotional intelligence (EQ) basically boils down to three basic traits: self-awareness, social awareness, and self-control

When it comes to emotional intelligence (EQ), it basically boils down to three basic traits: ***self-awareness, social awareness, and self-control***. For instance, in relationships, if you can read your partner's emotions, you can better predict what he or she might do next. While emotional intelligence is closely associated with personality traits, and personality traits are generally stable over time, they can also vary with context. Some individuals are more sensitive than others to contextual factors that may influence emotional understanding. For example, if a manager or supervisor is stressed, an employee may be more likely to misinterpret his or her boss' behavior or mood than an employee who is not in such a situation.

We live in a world of extremes. In the past, people thought that emotional intelligence was only the ability to pick up subtle nuances in your own emotions. There's a lot of people who are emotionally incompetent, and there's a lot of people who are emotionally intelligent. And it's probably fair to say that most of us fall somewhere in between. It is not a trait, it is a skill. It is something you can learn and improve upon. It has been said that emotional intelligence is what you need to get along in life. If you are intelligent, you can make sense of the world around you. You can understand other people, and even predict their behavior. But if you don't have emotional intelligence, you're out of luck.

If you have the ability to control your emotions, you can be emotionally competent. There's no question that emotional competence is one of the most important skills you can have in life. When we get angry, our emotions take over and we may act without thinking about the consequences of our actions.

Emotional incompetence makes us less effective communicators and leads to poor decision making.

Emotional intelligence is not something you're born with; it's something you can learn. It's important to be able to read the emotions of others, and when you can do this you'll understand a lot more about them than they do themselves. You will also be able to determine what is going on in their mind, and if you can make sense of their behavior, then you'll be able to predict their behavior, which is critical in a world of complexity.

When it comes to sales, emotional intelligence is more important than IQ.

That's the conclusion of a fascinating new study conducted by researchers at the **University of California**, **Berkeley** and **the University of Washington**.

In the study, participants were randomly assigned to one of three groups: The first group received a series of training sessions on how to improve their emotional intelligence (EI). The second group got similar training but was also taught how to improve their IQ. The third group did neither.

What did the study reveal?

The researchers found that people who improved their *emotional intelligence (EI)* were more effective at persuading others to buy things. People who improved their **IQ** were just as good at convincing people to do things as those in the control group.

So, while improving your IQ may be useful for certain tasks, it doesn't seem to be the key to success when it comes to selling.

Why is emotional intelligence so important?

The reason why emotional intelligence is so important is because people don't always choose what they want based on rational reasons. They often choose things because they feel emotionally attracted to them, not because they think about the pros and cons of the decision.

If you're a business owner, chances are your brain is full of brilliant ideas, and your heart is full of passion. But without emotional intelligence, you might not be able to bring those ideas to life. And if you don't bring them to life, your business might fail.

That's why it's essential to build emotional intelligence. If you don't have it, you can't fully leverage your brainpower and passion to create a thriving business that will thrive for years to come.

The good news is that building emotional intelligence is one of the most effective ways to improve yourself in every area of your life.

When you develop emotional intelligence, you become more patient, more flexible, more resilient, more creative, more focused, and more insightful. In short, you become better at living.

How to Identify the Emotional Needs of Your Customer, and How to Meet Them

Most business owners know they need to have a customer service plan, but many don't know how to identify the emotional needs of their customers. Customers have emotions, but it doesn't always come naturally for us to consider them. We think about customers' needs in terms of rational, logical decisions, and sometimes even neglect to do so. But what if there was another kind of need that was just as powerful and could be just as important to a customer's decision-making process?

According to research conducted by **IBS**, consumers need emotional fulfillment through shopping. They need to have a positive feeling about the purchase they're making, and they want to feel that the store or brand they're dealing with cares about them. The problem is that retailers tend to only serve the needs of the consumers, and not the other way around. They don't seem to realize that customers don't come to them for their products or services. They come for the emotional fulfillment. This means that when retailers create emotional fulfillment for the customer, they're doing business.

If you want to understand the emotional needs of your customer, you'll need to consider the following questions: <u>Is there something that scares them? Something that makes them laugh? Something that brings up anger or frustration? Anything that makes them feel warm inside?</u>

Anything that makes them sad or upset? What does your customer like about you? What makes them mad? What do they love about you?

Asking these questions will help you understand what makes your customers tick and then you can start to think about how to meet those needs.

When you are trying to sell something, you need to make sure that you are meeting the emotional needs of the customer. If they don't feel warm when they hear your product pitch, they are not going to buy it. They will say no. If you're looking to get a new customer, it's important to consider what makes them tick.

When someone is buying a car, they have their own set of emotions. Some people are worried about price, some are worried about safety and others are worried about the amount of money they can afford to spend on a new car. All of these emotions are important and it's up to you to find out what they are. Asking your customers what they like about your business is a great way to find out what makes them tick. If they love your service, then they are more likely to buy from you again.

If they don't love your service, it's time to figure out why.

Another way to find out what makes your customers tick is to ask them directly. You can use this method for a variety of reasons.

For example, if you're trying to get new customers, you might ask them what type of customer they would like to be. Do they want to be someone who pays full price or do they want to be a bargain shopper? If you have a retail location, then you can ask your customers what they like about the store. Do they like the colors? The layout? The prices? The atmosphere?

Another great way to find out what makes your customers tick is by asking them what they don't like about your business. This is a very powerful question, because it will allow you to find out what's not working. For example, if you run a restaurant, then you might ask your customers what they don't like about your food. Do they like the service? The prices? The portions? The taste?

At the end of the day, it's your goal to sell your product or service and turn your visitors into customers. You'll never get anywhere if you can't figure out what's working and what's not. But before you do anything else, you need to know who your ideal customer is. Who are you targeting?

Your website should be designed for one purpose: to attract potential customers. To do this, you must know who your ideal customers are.

If you can figure out what your customer likes about you, you can use that information to create a relationship with them. You can build trust. You can get them to talk to you more often, and spend more money. If you can figure out what your customer wants from you, you can give it to them. The only way to gain customers' loyalty is to first build trust in them. You do this by doing everything possible to treat them fairly and respectfully. It's important to remember that your customer doesn't know anything about you and your company. So the best you can do is to impress them with a good product.

There are three parts to emotional needs and you can identify it by studying carefully.
First, you must be aware that something is missing. Next, you must be aware that needs could be met. Finally, you must believe that a customer can afford to pay for the thing that satisfies their need.

That's what makes emotional needs compelling. This is a powerful tool, but it's not easy to figure out what your customers' emotional needs are.

The trick is knowing how you can fulfill their emotional needs and how you need to react to their needs as a human being, as well as your customer.

When you know what your customers' emotional needs are, it makes selling easier because you know what you need to do to satisfy them. Knowing what emotional needs your customers have, means that you know how you need to act in order to satisfy those needs.

Once you identify the need that drives a customer's purchase decision, the second step in the process is to determine the emotions that must be satisfied for the transaction to happen. This can be tricky because there is a lot of emotional variability in human beings. Some people might need the same thing in a very different way, and the same product can have completely different meanings and uses for different individuals.

The most common emotional needs that drive purchases are: pleasure, ***self-esteem, respect, loyalty, status, security, love****.*

The most common emotional needs that drive purchases are: *pleasure, self-esteem, respect, loyalty, status, security, love.* Understanding these are essential to selling because if you can figure out what a customer wants to satisfy an emotion, you know exactly how to sell to that person.

The last step is to find a way to satisfy the customer's emotional need. For example, when someone buys a pair of jeans, they are likely trying to satisfy one or more of these emotional needs:

Respect: Feeling like the person who wears these jeans is important to them.

Self-Esteem: Feeling good about themselves in the eyes of others.

Loyalty: Feeling that they have found a good value for their money.

Pleasure: Feeling satisfied with the purchase.

Security: Feeling safe and comfortable in the world.

Love: Feeling loved and appreciated by the other person.

The emotions that drive sales are different for every person and every sale, but all of these emotions must be addressed for a sale to happen.

Why is Emotional Intelligence Important?

Most people are aware of the fact that emotional intelligence is important. However, only 15% of people understand the importance of emotional intelligence. The link between emotional intelligence and leadership has been studied for decades. However, while most people have some sort of awareness of emotional intelligence, only a few understand what it really means and how it can help them lead more effectively.

Emotional intelligence is important and it can make or break your career. But why is emotional intelligence important? And how can it help you? It is very important for success and happiness. It gives us the ability to recognize our emotions and those around us.

People who understand their emotions and how they affect other people are better equipped to solve problems and make decisions. According to a research paper published in the International Journal of Wellbeing, emotional intelligence is related to improved performance and satisfaction at work, more successful romantic relationships, and increased self-esteem and happiness. There is no doubt that emotional intelligence is something that is beneficial to us as humans and it can be to your buisness too. EI has been linked with success in many fields: academics, marriage, sports, business, etc.

An entrepreneur should have an understanding of what motivates their audience and use this knowledge to drive engagement. An emotionally intelligent person understands their own emotions and those of others. They are aware of their own feelings and those of others. They can read situations and people and make informed decisions based on their knowledge of how they feel and why they feel the way they do.

To understand how the emotional side of selling influences our decisions, we need to first understand the role that emotion plays in decision-making. In other words, if we feel a certain way about something, we're more likely to choose to act in accordance with that feeling. That doesn't necessarily mean that the feeling itself is bad or good, but rather that our emotions influence us to act.

When people are successful in life, they're successful because they manage their emotions well. An emotionally intelligent person knows how to manage her own emotions. They understand that emotions can take over a person when they aren't managed well. Emotional intelligence is also closely linked to physical health. Emotionally intelligent people tend to be more physically active and healthier than others.

Most people want to be happy, but some people want to be smart. People who want to be smart tend to focus on factual evidence to support their claims, while people who want to be happy tend to look for emotional evidence. This is why emotional intelligence is so valuable. People who are smart understand the importance of understanding others and have the ability to empathize with those around them.

EI is important in regards to self-awareness and understanding what motivates you. For example, if you're really hungry, you'll eat anything — even if it's gross — just so you don't feel hungry anymore. On the other hand, if you're really passionate about something you want to eat, you may cook it or find a way to get it just because you love doing it.

How to Develop Emotional Intelligence Skills?

The skills of *emotional intelligence (EI)* are the core competencies of the human brain that enable us to communicate with others. These skills can be measured by abilities such as, the ability to read people, listen effectively, be mindful, and maintain self-awareness.

One of the most important business skills for success is - an example of a business owner, such person would build a company that doesn't make rash decisions. They are patient and careful in their dealings, and they make sure that the business is properly built up before taking any rash actions. The company is willing to wait until its employees are fully confident about a certain decision before making the final call. As such, it's worth exploring how we can all learn to become better listeners, observers, and more aware of our emotions and feelings.

In the past few years, we've seen a growing number of companies using social media and social technology to connect with customers and build long-term relationships. Many people argue that this strategy is becoming more and more important, but how exactly do you do it? One of the major keys to making these interactions more than just a passing fad is empathy. Empathy is the ability to understand someone else's emotional experience and be able to convey that understanding back to them in a positive way. People with more emotional intelligence have been shown to be more successful in business, and they're much easier to deal with.

So, *how do you develop the ability to empathize?*

For example, a study found that the most successful **CEOs** possess high levels of emotional intelligence. If you want to become a better leader and more effective communicator, develop your emotional intelligence skills.

Emotional intelligence skills are often overlooked by individuals and organizations. The reason for this is that people tend to focus on tangible skills such as logical reasoning, math, and language. In contrast, emotional intelligence has been deemed a less important skill in the workplace than cognitive intelligence. However, this thinking is outdated.

Today, it's possible to develop emotional intelligence skills in ways that have never before been possible. This might sound silly to some, but developing emotional intelligence skills is very valuable to business. Business people who demonstrate high levels of emotional intelligence are better able to solve problems, handle conflicts, and communicate effectively. Those without emotional intelligence skills often fail to read others' emotions, are unable to accurately gauge others' moods, and struggle to get along with co-workers and superiors.

To improve your emotional intelligence, practice ***self-awareness***. The ability to understand your own emotions is a big part of emotional intelligence. If you're not aware of your own emotions, it's hard to understand others' emotions. You can do this by simply observing your feelings, which is known as *"self-observation."* When you notice that you're feeling sad or angry, try to determine why you're feeling this way. What happened to bring on this emotion? You can also practice self-observation by keeping a journal.

Another principle is ***emotion control***, which is a fancy way of saying that we can control our emotions. By being able to master your emotions, you can improve your relationship with other people. Emotional intelligence is important for your career success, and you can apply some of these skills in the workplace. If you're a manager, you can influence the emotions of your subordinates.

If you're an employee, you can influence the emotions of your boss. Emotions are very powerful. If you're feeling negative, you will often attract negative events into your life. On the other hand, if you're feeling positive, you will attract positive events into your life. This is one of the reasons why it's so important to learn how to control your emotions. EI can help you better navigate situations, predict outcomes, and achieve your goals. It doesn't matter if you're in a relationship or at work, being emotionally intelligent can help you communicate effectively, develop better friendships and relationships, handle conflict better, and more.

If you're interested in developing emotional intelligence skills in your business or personal life, consider taking some time to reflect on the emotional state you're in right now. What kind of mood are you in? What are you feeling? What are you thinking? Where are you? How does your emotional state impact your day-to-day actions, decisions, and interactions? How can you take steps to improve your emotional state today?

If you don't know your strengths or weaknesses, you can't develop emotional intelligence. To help improve their emotional intelligence skills, the employees took a test that measured the four dimensions of emotional intelligence *(emotional self-awareness, the ability to manage emotions in oneself and others, the ability to understand emotions in oneself and others, and the ability to respond effectively to emotion)*. The results showed that the higher a company's level of emotional intelligence, the better the employee relationships and performance, and the lower the turnover rate.

The results were even more remarkable when it came to job satisfaction. Employees who were rated higher in emotional intelligence had a higher level of job satisfaction, and they also reported having fewer health problems. When employees were asked what they liked most about their jobs, they reported having the opportunity to interact with customers. You may be surprised to learn that some companies are using emotional intelligence training for their employees. These include a global insurance company that provided training to help employees identify their own strengths and weaknesses, and an oil company that gave emotional intelligence training to its new hires.

To develop emotional intelligence, you need to practice a number of skills such as:

- Pay attention to your emotions and your feelings
- Understand your feelings and those of others
- Use your emotions to improve your relationships with other people
- Learn to use your emotions to help solve problems.

If you don't know your strengths or weaknesses, you can't develop emotional intelligence.

The best way to find out is to take a personality test, such as the **Myers-Briggs Type Indicator (MBTI)**. This test will help you discover your personality type, which will also help you to understand your strengths and weaknesses.

There are four main personality types:

- **Introverts** – prefer to spend time alone with their thoughts, ideas, and activities.
- **Extroverts** – prefer to spend time with others, and enjoy being around others.

- **Sensors** – are highly perceptive, and pay attention to details.
- **Judgers** – are highly critical, and focus on rules and regulations.

How do I know my personality type?

You can take an online test for free at www.MyersBriggs.com. There are also paper versions of the test that you can take at your local library or book store. After taking the test, you will receive a report which will tell you your personality type, along with your strengths and weaknesses.

Deliberate Practice of Emotional Intelligence

If you want to be more emotionally intelligent, you need to put deliberate practice into it. To develop the ability to read people and discern their emotions, take some time to practice looking at people without judgement.

We spend a lot of time reading the social cues of others but rarely stop to examine our own emotions and reactions. The concept of emotional intelligence can be traced back to research published by Mayer-Johnson in

1990. The goal is to make sure that you understand how your customers and potential customers feel about a particular issue or decision.

By understanding what they're feeling, you can better predict their behavior, which will help you to be more effective at closing sales. This is especially true in the case of service professionals, like doctors and dentists. They have to be able to read people and get them to trust them enough to reveal their most personal information. Emotional Intelligence is a set of skills that we all possess to varying degrees. But just because you have them doesn't mean that you're using them effectively.

You might have the ability to read people, but if you don't know what to say or do next, then you're not using your emotional intelligence. You can also use emotional intelligence in your sales conversations. If you notice that a customer has become defensive or angry, you can ask them questions that will help them feel better about themselves. By asking open-ended questions, you give them something to think about and feel more positive about themselves. In the end, this will lead to higher retention rates and higher profits.

Deliberate practice of emotional intelligence in business can be by using our emotional intelligence as a filter and gatekeeper to how we approach problems, making us better at handling the daily stresses and pressures of life. When it comes to emotions, I think most people assume that because they have them, their boss is going to love them. It's true that people who are emotionally intelligent understand how their emotions and theirs colleagues affect the environment, but this doesn't mean that they should expect to walk into a business meeting and instantly make themselves feel more important, or more respected.

So; how do we tap into our emotional intelligences? Below are steps to harnessing emotional intelligence in business.

- **Learning:** To become emotionally intelligent, we must develop empathy.
- **Developing self-awareness:** Emotions are only expressed through thoughts, words, and behaviors, hence it is important to be self-aware. Being self-aware and reflective is very appreciable. When you get angry, first take a step back and assess what's

going on. You may be reacting to something that has nothing to do with you. If so, don't beat yourself up about it. You're not responsible for someone else's actions, or for the outcome of an interaction. You are only responsible for your own behavior.

- Understanding how our emotions influence our decision-making.
- **Taking action:** Take ownership of your actions, and learn to take responsibility. If you're struggling to control your emotions in the workplace, the best advice is to simply take a break. Walk around the block. Call someone you care about. Read a book. Do something physical. Get some fresh air.
- **Grow:** The journey to emotional intelligence is a lifelong endeavor. You can only get better everyday if you allow yourself to grow.
- Lastly, **practice gratitude:** When you practice gratitude, you begin to appreciate the good things in your life, and also see them as gifts from the universe rather than things you have to work hard to get. This helps you to be more positive, more tolerant of others and less judgmental, and it reduces stress and depression.

Chapter 2

How to Identify Your Customer's Emotional Style

A great way to understand why customers shop online or offline is to understand what motivates them emotionally. We live in a world where people are constantly being sold to, and it's becoming harder and harder to get noticed, and make a positive impact in people's lives. For example, if you're selling high-end products, then you need to focus on the "high end" customers, not the "lower end" customers.

A huge part of successful sales involves identifying your customer's emotional style. A strong understanding of what makes a person tick and what causes them to act in certain ways is the key to understanding how to communicate effectively with them.

Emotional style *is the ability to process feelings in different ways.* It's an important psychological trait to understand because it determines how you respond to different emotional situations, how you express yourself, and ultimately how you approach everyday life. There are three emotional styles: ***the rational, the intuitive, and the instinctive.***

The rational style is analytical, logical, and objective; it requires an ability to look at problems from every angle and come up with a solution. The intuitive style is more holistic and fluid; it's based on feeling and intuition. And the instinctive style is based on body language and physical reactions.

In the business world, the rational style tends to be more productive, while the intuitive and instinctive styles tend to be more creative.

Emotional style is one of the biggest factors in determining your overall productivity

Emotional style is one of the biggest factors in determining your overall productivity. For example, if you're a rational person, you'll need to practice emotional control in order to get things done. You may have trouble expressing feelings, which can lead to anger or frustration. Your emotions will also affect your decision-making, so you'll have to learn to separate yourself from them.

On the other hand, if you're an intuitive person, you'll need to work on learning how to be more objective and detached from the situation in order to make better decisions. A good example of this is someone who's a highly emotional, passionate person. If something doesn't go his way, he'll be in a rage. And because he's a very strong person, he'll take it out on others as well. He can't let anyone else have an opinion or perspective that differs from his own. So; if you're around him, and don't agree with him about something, you better watch your back. You might find yourself in the middle of a fight over nothing at all.

In general, people who are more logical and less emotional tend to make better decisions. But since this is not always the case, you'll need to develop both sides of your brain in order to make better decisions.

There are two types of emotions: *positive and negative.* The difference between them is that one is beneficial and the other is detrimental. There's a reason we have emotions at all. We need them. They are essential to our survival. They motivate us to do things like get up and go to work, and they also help us to learn from mistakes and develop empathy. When they're in balance, we are better people. But when they're too strong, they can be detrimental. We all know people who seem to be constantly upset. They're angry or anxious most of the time. They're not happy and their happiness is out of proportion to what they have. Or they're always sad. They just can't seem to find peace of mind. The problem with emotions is that they can get stuck.

If you've ever been in an argument with someone who's too emotional to listen, or if you've ever had a conversation with someone who never seems to be able to let it go, then you know how hard it is to talk to someone who has a problem regulating their emotions. It can be very frustrating.

When you have an emotion stuck, you can be stuck with it. You can feel like your emotions are out of control. It can be really difficult to think about the future because you're so focused on the past. It can be really hard to take action because your feelings keep getting in the way. When you have an emotion stuck, it can be almost impossible to feel good. You might think that if you just change something, your emotions will disappear. Maybe you'll change your relationship with your parents. Or maybe you'll change your job. But your emotions won't disappear. They will come back, and they'll stick around for a long time after you've changed things. Your emotions are part of you. They don't go away when you change something. They come back. And they stay stuck with you until you deal with them.

What does this mean?

It means that when you have an emotion stuck, you can't just change something and get rid of it. You have to figure out what it is and what you can do about it. How do you know if you have an emotion stuck?

If you feel like you can't do anything about a certain problem or if you find yourself saying over and over again: *"I hate it. I just hate it,"* then you probably have an emotion stuck. Here are some of the things that may be sticking around in your emotions: You may be stuck with a negative feeling because you think it's permanent. For example, if you're afraid that your life will never change, then you're stuck with that feeling. But you don't have to live in fear; you can change your thinking to believe that everything changes and that you can always move forward. You may be stuck with an emotion that you're afraid to face. For example, if you're afraid of feeling lonely, then you're stuck with that feeling. But you don't have to live in fear; you can change your thinking to believe that you can connect with other people and that you're not alone.

You may be stuck with an emotion that makes you feel like a failure or that you don't deserve good things. For example, if you feel like a failure when someone else gets a promotion or a raise, then you're stuck with that feeling. But you don't have to live in failure; you can change your thinking to believe that you can get promoted someday and that you do deserve good things.

If you find yourself stuck with an emotion that you know is harmful to you, then you may need to work on changing your thoughts. If you think you're stuck because you believe you're unlovable, for example, then you may want to change your thoughts.

Most marketers believe that they know their customers. This is true when you're talking about demographics, income level, or even age. But what about emotional style? What if you could actually tell what kind of person is buying your product or service? What if you could pinpoint which emotional types are most likely to buy from you?

Six styles that tend to dominate our emotions are: the pursuer, the avoider, the influencer, the collaborator, the controller, and the nurturer

To know your audience, you must understand your customer's emotional style. While we all have some degree of emotional intelligence, there are six styles that tend to dominate our emotions: *the pursuer, the avoider, the influencer, the collaborator, the controller, and the nurturer.*

Once you identify your customers' emotional style, it becomes easier to understand their wants and needs. When you know this, you can build more powerful communication tools to connect with them on a deeper level.

If you were to ask people which emotional style is the most dominant, they would probably say **"the pursuer.** " This type is always looking to get what they want. They are constantly in motion and seek to be in control of situations. They are constantly wanting to be right. They want to win every time.

"The avoider" is the exact opposite. They do not care about being right. They do not care about being the one who wins. They are content to go along for the ride. They enjoy the ride. They simply want to feel good about themselves and be accepted.

"The influencer" is the middle-ground. They are somewhere between the pursuer and the avoider. They like to influence others and they want to have influence over others. They enjoy being able to get things done because they have the ability to persuade others to do what they want them to do. They also enjoy being in control. They are not interested in the outcome of an endeavor. They only want to know that they were a part of it. They want to feel important. They want to be the center of attention. They want to be noticed. They want people to look at them and say, "I'm glad you did that for me." A lot of these influencers can't take rejection. It hurts their feelings. A lot of them can't handle criticism or being told no. They have to be right. And if they are not right, they will not change their opinion or belief.

If you want to be an effective influencer, you need to understand the difference between your ideal customer and the real customers that are already in your customer base.

When you sell a product, people who can afford that product will typically spend more on it than people who can't afford it. In other words, you need to sell to the people who have the most money. That doesn't mean that the people who can afford it aren't important. The point is that they represent the most potential buyers for your products. You'll never be able to convert every single one of them into customers, but if you can turn some of them into loyal customers, then you're going to do much better than if you focus only on the people who can't afford it. If you're selling something expensive, like an iPad or an iPhone, you'll want to focus on the people who can afford it.

When you're trying to figure out whether a product is a match for a particular consumer's emotional style, look at the colors the person uses in their home. Certain colors will work well for someone with a creative personality because these colors allow the user to express themselves through the design.

However, some colors are better suited for people who are more reserved or logical. For example, if you want to sell a product to a conservative buyer, use gray and white. However, if you want to appeal to a more extroverted individual, use brighter colors, like green and orange.

While emotional style is not something that marketers should obsess over, it is something that every marketer needs to be aware of, especially if they're trying to target a specific emotional style. We all have emotional styles; some people are more likely to be extroverts while others are more likely to be introverts. Each emotional style has unique behavioral tendencies, but the general rule is that people who fall into certain emotional styles are more likely to behave in certain ways when it comes to marketing messages.

Engaging Your Customers with the Right Message at the Right Time

The best way to engage your customers is by offering them value, providing useful information, and showing them what they want.

The best way to engage your customers is by offering them value

Your customers are on the go, and you can make their lives

easier by providing them with a variety of choices—from the food they eat to the type of car they drive to the clothes they wear. This can offer a great customer experience that drives repeat purchases, and customer loyalty, even if you're a one-person shop.

Six phases of customer engagement cycle are; Awareness, Interest, Desire, Action, Loyalty, and Advocacy.

In my years of working in marketing, I've learned that the customer engagement cycle can be broken into six phases: *Awareness, Interest, Desire, Action, Loyalty, and Advocacy*.

These phases take place in different ways in different stages of the buying process. The problem is that most marketers focus only on a couple of these phases at any given time. But if you really understand how each phase works, you'll have a better chance of creating long-term relationships with your customers.

The first phase is ***awareness***. This is the moment when you reach out to the potential customer. With a mobile-first strategy, your messages and ads will be sent to users' phones and tablets first. In this way, you're better able to reach consumers at the times and places they spend their time most. Whether it's through direct mail, email, or a website, you want to get the attention of the person and create an interest in what you have to offer. This is the first step to the other five phases.

When you're reaching out to someone, don't bombard them with sales messages. You want to give them something they find valuable and interesting. For example, you could have a monthly newsletter where you provide valuable information and insights into your product or service. If you're marketing to a large group, you can segment the people you're contacting based on their interests. Also, you could send a newsletter to a group of people who have a similar interest e.g football. If you're selling a product, this could be as simple as showing them a video about your product.

The next step is ***interest***. This is when you get the potential customer to stop reading your email and click on your message. It's when you've got them hooked on what you have to say and want to know more. This means that you need to understand the importance of using the right words and delivering that message in the right tone of voice because this can help your persuasiveness.

Another phase is ***desire***. This is when a person has an interest or curiosity about a product or service. It could be because he has read about it in a magazine, heard a friend talk about it, or even seen it on television. He or she may have a need for the product or service, such as a new car, a house, or even a vacation. *The principle of persuasion can come in handy here.* The idea behind it is simple: Your message needs to address your customer's goals. The most effective way to persuade someone to buy what you sell is to address his or her goals. If you're selling a car, for example, you need to address the customer's needs, wants, and goals. You can use this information to determine which messages are most likely to get through to your customer. For example, you might say something like, *"The Ford Mustang is a great value, but the Dodge Challenger is even better."* When you have identified your customer's goals, you then need to use the principles of persuasion to help persuade him or her.

Action, Loyalty, and Advocacy are ways to speed up the buying process and they all happen. Let's continue with the typical car situation: When the buyer has decided to buy a new car. They proceed to a dealership and get into an actual salesperson's car. He or she asks you if you'd like to test drive the vehicle. That is, the salesman will take you for a ride around the parking lot in your own car. Then he or she will invite you back to the office to discuss the sale. That is where the *Loyalty step* comes in. The dealership has done its job of presenting you with a great vehicle. It has also done its part of establishing a good relationship with you. Now it is time to do its part of the deal and make sure you are happy with the car you've chosen. This is the *Advocacy step*. The more steps we can take to speed up the buying process the better.

According to the theory of planned behavior, the key to success is finding a way to engage your audience. You should create content that engages them in a way that motivates them to act on your message. But keep in mind that if you have a product or service that has been used by many people before, you can probably be rest assured that people who have tried it will remember the reasons why they bought it, if it met their need, and why they like it. Howeever, if the product was bad they will remember the negative aspects of the experience, like whether or not it worked for them and the level of effort they needed to put in to make it work.

How to Increase Customer Loyalty

The best way to keep customers coming back is to find out what they want, and deliver it. There is only one place you should be spending your time. *Not on marketing, but on customer service.* You can't spend more time with your customers than you're already spending, but you can spend more time with them than anyone else. And that's what you need to do if you want to increase customer loyalty. It's no secret that customer loyalty is important, but how do you make sure it stays at its highest level?

Most people will stay loyal to a company if they like its products and services. But many people are also loyal to a company because of its brand. Brand loyalty is a huge driver of sales. A brand is an intangible value that people will pay money to buy into. It has been found that the most successful businesses are those that maintain a consistent brand experience over multiple touchpoints, including email, websites, customer service, marketing, sales, etc. These businesses understand that customers are always looking for a brand experience that feels personal, helpful, friendly and relevant.

In fact, according to a recent survey, 68% of people who bought a product online did so because it made them feel valued and appreciated. It is easy to persuade someone if you can provide a reason to believe that something is valuable to them. This is why customer loyalty schemes are so effective: they offer a clear value proposition, and tell people why they should stick with a certain brand. If they provide a reason to believe that they will get value out of doing so, then they will.

A customer loyalty program is one of the oldest methods used to increase customer retention. While there are different types of loyalty programs, one of the most popular types is the loyalty card. It is usually attached to an existing purchase or subscription, and offers some sort of reward for frequent and consistent purchases.

Some examples of rewards include *discounts, freebies, or gift cards*. By increasing customer retention, a company has a higher likelihood of turning a profit and staying in business. However, a loyalty program needs to be implemented carefully to be effective and beneficial to the customers. Loyalty programs aren't just about getting customers to spend more money. If they were, then there wouldn't be such a powerful sales tool. These programs are designed to keep customers coming back, and to create customer relationships that feel special. They're built on trust, so they rely on being transparent and honest about what customers are getting and how they're using it.

Another important principle is ***social proof.*** Social proof is based on the idea that people are influenced by what others are doing. So; <u>if you have majority believe in your product, you can increase the likelihood of people patronizing you. If people perceive that your brand has a positive reputation for honesty, reliability, and value, then they'll be more likely to buy from you and keep buying from you</u>. *The best thing you can do for your customers is to deliver on your promise, and in return they'll reward you with customer loyalty.*

How To Increase Customer Retention

It's no secret that customer retention is one of the biggest challenges that most small businesses face. We all know people who leave our company or our clients because of poor service, but there's a deeper problem at play. People often leave bad bosses, or the wrong boss altogether. So *what does that mean?*

It means that if you're going to have good, long-term success, you need to be willing to make changes. It means that if you think your business is already "good," you've got a problem. Your current customers aren't happy, so there's a good chance that they aren't loyal. If they aren't loyal, they're leaving. And without loyal customers, your business isn't going anywhere. It's a simple concept, but if you're looking for help with customer retention and customer loyalty, that's what this portion is here for.

Retention is crucial for any kind of customer relationship management system. Many online retailers say they are committed to customer retention but in reality, most retailers struggle with keeping customers coming back time and time again. In fact, there are several products and services to create a sustainable business. Some businesses struggle even after investing tons of money in advertising campaigns hoping to get more customers but customers keep leaving. You've been through it before right?

There are plenty of factors that affect customer retention: *location, products offered, price, ease of use, and so on.*

But no matter how big or small your business is, *one factor that can help you increase customer retention is the quality of your customer service*. After all, your customers expect a certain level of customer service from you — whether it be through email, social media or telephone.

There are many ways to increase customer retention, but the most common methods include keeping customers informed of *upcoming events, special offers, and promotions*. The key is to do this in a timely manner that fits the individual customer's needs.

Another way to increase customer retention is to make your product as easy and fun to use as possible. The less friction there is for your customers to use your product, the better it will be. Make sure that all the features of your product are clearly visible and easy to use. When it comes to payment options, make it as simple as possible for customers to choose their preferred method, but don't offer too many.

In general, the longer customers remain with a company, the more likely they are to become loyal, repeat customers.

The Art of Empathy and its Effect on Customer Loyalty

To create a customer experience that people will remember, you must take a honest look at yourself and your company. That is how you can become a more effective communicator with customers and prospects. If you want to build trust with your customers, you have to start by listening to them. You have to start by caring about their needs. This is the very essence of empathy, which can help you to understand what makes your customers tick. Empathy is not only essential to a good work relationship with your customer, but it's also vital to a healthy and satisfying customer experience.

The idea behind empathy is to make the customer feel like you're talking directly to him or her. The key to connect and empathize with such person is by speaking his or her language. At the heart of any business relationship is in need for empathy. This is the ability to put yourself in someone else's shoes and relate to them. To a certain extent, this ability is innate and comes naturally. But understanding and applying it in the workplace goes beyond empathy. This is the art of empathy, and it's critical for both the individual and the company. It means being able to listen and understand the customer's needs and desires and helping the customer feel appreciated.

A great piece of advice I have for you is to *"empathize with your customer."* The concept was simple. But, it's surprisingly difficult to do. Most people can empathize with themselves or their friends or family. But, very few people can really put themselves into the shoes of another person who's trying to make a purchase decision. The reason for this is simple. Most of us only really care about ourselves. So, even if you feel like you know what your customers are going through, and why they're making the purchase decision they're making, you still have to try to put yourself in their shoes and understand their motivations, goals, and frustrations before you can begin to provide value to them.

This is how you start to create empathy with your customers. The first step is to try to understand what their current situation is. This can be a bit difficult, especially when you're dealing with a complex sale. That's because many customers aren't aware of the fact that they're trying to make a purchase decision at all. In other words, they think that they're just doing business with you, and that the transaction is just a formality.

In order to get around this problem, we need to understand that people don't really make decisions like they're doing business. Instead, they're trying to find a solution to a problem or solve an issue. And, when they're buying from you, they're trying to do so in a way that best suits their needs.

So, to begin to understand your customers better, it's important to ask yourself these questions:

- What are their problems?
- What are their goals?
- Why does he/she need my product?
- What are their frustrations?
- Why is he/she frustrated?
- Why are they making the purchase decision they are?
- What problems does my customer have?
- How does he/she feel about them?
- Why is my customer buying from me?
- What can I do to help my customer solve his/her problem?
- Is there anything else I should know about my customer?

To help you answer these questions, try this exercise:

Think about the last time you purchased something. What were you thinking about when you decided to buy? Was it the price, was it the design, was it the features? Did you even consider how much you liked the product or service? Think about what you were doing when you made that decision. If you're like most people, you were probably trying to solve a problem. You were looking for a solution. To get people to share your brand story, you have to show them that you understand them and their challenges.

How to Build Rapport with Customers

When people meet, they don't just look at each other - they're also reading each other's body language, gestures, and facial expressions.

If your smile is too wide, for example, you're likely to be perceived as a friendly person who's happy to be meeting someone new. But if you're frowning or have a grimace on your face, you might come across as an unfriendly person who doesn't want to meet people.

Similarly, when you're looking at someone, you're also reading their facial expressions. If their eyebrows are raised, it may mean that they're interested in what you're saying.

When we first meet someone, we often subconsciously read their body language and gestures. The more we do this, the easier it becomes to understand them, and the better we get at reading each other. So when you're meeting someone for the first time, try to use your best body language skills to make a good impression.

You'll need to pay attention to:

How you're standing - Are you leaning forward or back? Are you standing straight, or slouching? Your posture - Is your head held high, or do you look down at the floor?

Your facial expression - What kind of expression are you giving off? Do you have a smile on your face?

When it comes to building rapport with customers, many companies and marketers focus on the need for *face-to-face meetings*. But while in-person is still the most powerful way to build relationships with potential clients, technology is disrupting the traditional in-person meeting.

"The secret to creating rapport is to be genuine." It

doesn't matter if you are being yourself or whether your personality is a little bit on the intense side; the point is to be authentic. Show your customers you really care about them by being honest.

When you're building rapport with your customers, there are three big reasons to do so.

First, building rapport with customers helps to make them feel more confident and comfortable with your brand.

Second, establishing rapport can help you build trust with your customers. When you're sending an emails to your customers, start every email or message with a simple greeting like "Hi!" and don't get too fancy with your salutations. This simple gesture helps customers feel like they're interacting with a human being instead of an impersonal robot.

And third, it'll help to foster a relationship between you and your customers.

Rapport is all about understanding your customers and

providing them with a level of trust. It’s about understanding their values, needs, preferences, and lifestyles. If you’re interested in becoming a successful influencer in buisness, you’ll need to build rapport with your followers by consistently sharing value and content they care about. This will allow you to connect with your audience, and gain their trust.

Knowing and Understanding the Customer's Personality Traits

A personality test allows you to understand how to approach marketing to customers based on how they operate. Knowing someone’s personality traits helps you better understand how to talk to them. Each person's personality comes with specific strengths and weaknesses. When you know someone’s personality, you can tailor your marketing efforts to fit their particular needs. An interesting psychological concept that is relevant to ecommerce is the concept of personality traits. A person's personality traits can be measured by using personality tests, which can reveal details about how customers behave and react to certain stimuli. For instance, people who tend to be more impulsive are more likely to purchase online than those who are more calculated.

Understanding customer personality traits is an essential part of any marketing plan. Knowing the type of person you're selling to and having the ability to speak their language will ensure that you reach out to them effectively.

When we're looking at the different personality traits of customers, we have to take into account the kind of customers that are most likely to visit our store. Knowing their personality traits will help us figure out if they're a *"doer"* or a *"thinker." "Doers"* are usually risk takers, and tend to enjoy being active, while *"thinkers"* are risk averse, and often like to spend time alone.

Let's define what it means to be a *"doer" or a "thinker."*

A doer is someone who enjoys doing things. They may be a risk taker, but they still like to get things done. Doers are people who are always on the go and love to get things done. They have no problem getting their hands dirty. They want to get things done as quickly as possible. They love to work on projects and see them through to completion. The downside of this personality trait is that doers may take on too many projects at once. Doers tend to get overwhelmed easily. They have a hard time managing their time, and they can become distracted by the day-to-day tasks. When they're not working, they're usually thinking about work.

Thinkers are more likely to be the people who enjoy spending time alone. They may enjoy working alone or with other *"thinkers"* as long as there's something to think about. They like to think about things. They like to ponder over things. They like to learn new things. They're always coming up with new ideas and trying to figure out what they want to do next. Thinkers can be introverted and quiet. They can also be extremely extroverted and talkative.

We live in an age where consumers are empowered, and are using the internet to research and compare prices and purchase products online, so it's no longer a good strategy to focus on the product itself. Instead, businesses must understand what makes their customers tick, and create products or services to match that personality trait.

Let's discuss the different types of personalities and how you can best cater your brand to suit the unique needs of each.

Understanding Personality Types

There is no one "type" of person who buys from you – everyone has their own set of needs, desires, and expectations. In fact, a recent study by **Forbes** found that there are over 1,000 personality traits which make up our personalities, but here are some of the most common:

Analytical: They like things in order, logical, and don't want to waste time or money.

Creative: They like to be free and spontaneous, they love to create art and enjoy being innovative. They are highly sensitive, emotional, and need to feel appreciated.

Social: They like to talk about themselves and enjoy the company of others. They enjoy giving advice and help others. They are usually good listeners and great at making connections with people.

Detail Oriented: They like things organized and in order, they hate waste and prefer things to be done perfectly.

Spirited: They like action and adventure, they are strong-willed and independent.

Intuitive: They are good at reading other people and can easily tell what someone is thinking or feeling. They love to listen and are very empathetic.

Introverted: They enjoy being alone and are good at thinking. They like to have quiet times and to focus on a task.

Extroverted: They enjoy interacting with others and enjoy talking about themselves. They love to socialize and will do anything for attention.

How You Can Best Cater Your Brand to Suit the Unique Needs of Your Customers

Catering to your brand is one of the most important parts of running a successful business. It's also a difficult thing to do because catering to your brand means catering to each individual client, which can be challenging if you're not careful. We're going to take a look at how you can best cater your brand to suit the unique needs of each. You'll notice that we talk about branding. The reason for this is because branding is essential to your business and should be the number one priority.

If you're not branding, then you're not doing your job. When you're catering to your brand, it's important to remember that every client will have their own needs. Some clients may want something simple, while others may want something more extravagant. You'll need to cater to each individual client as they come to you and make sure that you're meeting their needs.

It's important that you're not just catering to them because they're your client. You should be catering to them because you're a great caterer who wants to create beautiful and memorable experiences for all of their clients.

Recognizing and Appreciating the Different Needs of Customers

If you want to really stand out, you need to understand the individual needs and motivations of your target audience, especially if you want to sell high ticket items. If you know the typical reasons why someone will buy a particular product, you'll know how to tailor your pitch accordingly.

The second psychology principle is the need for variety. People want different things. They want what is comfortable, what they know, and what makes them happy. These needs, however, are not mutually exclusive; people often want all three.

We all have different needs and desires. We have different motivations, concerns, goals, and desires. And these differences drive us to behave differently, buy differently, respond differently. It's the differences between our different needs that give rise to the different actions, reactions, and behaviors we take. There’s no single reason for why we buy something. It’s a combination of our needs and what we desire. We don’t necessarily want what we need. Sometimes, we don’t even need what we want. For example, some people buy products for the thrill of the hunt, but others buy them to impress their friends.

When a business fails to recognize the unique needs of its customers, it ends up delivering the wrong product. A great example of a business that understands the needs of their customers is **Amazon**. Amazon knows that their customers want to shop, but they also know that they want to do it quickly. Amazon sells a lot of products, and they have thousands of them available at any given time. But Amazon's biggest differentiator isn't having a large selection—it's offering fast delivery. Amazon offers free 2 day shipping for everything in the store, and Prime members receive free shipping on items over $35 and free next-day shipping on items over $25. Amazon also offers expedited shipping and returns.

What you need to do is identify who your target audience is, and understand the unique needs and goals that they have. There are certain key points in any customer journey that you need to pay attention to, but you also need to recognize that not every customer has the same experience when they're interacting with you online. Some need more guidance than others, and they might not be the ones who need to be persuaded the most. Instead, those customers who don't fit into your specific marketing goals might not be the best candidates to be persuaded in the first place.

The final stage of this process is the pricing of your product or service. Once you have your product or service figured out, then pricing it is easy. You can create a website and use a tool like **Google Adwords, Facebook Ads, LinkedIn Ads, Twitter Ads, Instagram Ads,** etc. to run ads on it to make money from the sale of your product or service. This takes the stress out of pricing your company's products as you don't have to worry about finding the right price point that makes sense for you.

Knowing Your Customers' Motivations

Answering this question is a critical step towards creating compelling content for your audience. The good news is that you don't have to be a psychologist to figure this one out, but if you are a psychologist, this is the best place to start. The answers to this question will give you insight into your audience's motivations and how they want to be treated. By understanding these motivations, you'll be able to come up with content that will appeal to your customers. It's not enough to understand why people are buying what you're selling. You must also know why they aren't.

People make decisions for a variety of reasons, and the easiest way to get a grasp on why they make the choices they do is to understand what they're looking for. Once you know this, you'll have a much better understanding of who your ideal customers are and what makes them tick.

Understanding your customers' motivations can help you identify and target their needs.

If your goal is to persuade someone to buy from you, you need to know what drives their decisions. This is especially true if you want them to buy from you over competitors. For instance, if your company offers something like a subscription service, then you should know why people are more likely to sign up for a monthly plan than a yearly one. Knowing your customers' motivations can be tricky, but knowing why they act as they do is essential to getting your business off the ground.

For ecommerce retailers, the biggest advantage of urgency is that it's cost-free. There is no upfront cost to build urgency around any given product or service. Urgency can be built around anything you sell online. It can be built around a promotion or discount; a free trial or offer; a free shipping deal or promo code; and much more. However, it's usually more effective when it's built around a time-based sale or offer.

For example, if you sell a product or service that costs $100, it's better to build urgency around a promotion where you give customers 10% off their purchase. This is because people will have to make a decision very quickly. If they can't make the decision, they'll likely choose someone who has a larger discount. **A/B testing** is a great way to optimize for conversions.

Building Customer Relationships

Customer relationships and repeat business are much harder than they seem. It's true that customers come back because they love the product or service. But in most cases, it's because they feel that they have a relationship with someone in the company who cares about them, and wants to help them succeed. To build relationships with your customers, you need to give them something in return for them caring enough about your brand to contact you again. You can start building relationships with your customers today by doing something kind for them. Don't forget to thank them when you make a sale.

The second tip to consider is to give your customers some of the benefits of using your product. Offer to give them a discount, free shipping, or free trial, but offer something only if you get to keep the business. Be flexible, too. For example, a customer may request free shipping on a particular item, but if you are having trouble keeping up with demand, you can offer the same deal on another item, or even a third.

Creating a Loyal Client Base

One of the keys to having a profitable business is in knowing who your loyal customers are and developing repeat business with them. Loyalty, in this case, means someone who knows your products and services well and makes a habit out of patronizing your business. They'll visit you time and again, and even refer their friends and family to you. *Having loyal customers is a key component of building a successful business.*

For instance, some writers often forget that the majority of people who read their content don't do so because they're looking for something specific. Instead, they're simply passing through and enjoying the ride. They're looking for entertainment, inspiration, and some kind of feeling of fulfillment, whether it's positive or negative. This is why it's so important to offer content that appeals to people at various stages of life. You'll want to cater to people who are interested in learning about the latest trends, to those who are seeking inspiration for creative ideas, and to those who are seeking answers to specific problems. And, of course, you need to have content that offers guidance to anyone with questions about how to run their business effectively.

People are more likely to return to a store or restaurant that has treated them well in the past, but you can create loyal customers by treating all your clients well. When you think about it, it's really hard to be loyal to someone who treats you poorly. It's easy to become a loyal client when you're satisfied with your service. So, it's best to have a few options and services that you can provide and stick with the one that's the best for you and your client. You can do this in a number of ways.

- Provide incentives to current customers.
- Use testimonials and endorsements to demonstrate the value of your products and services.
- Send promotional emails to remind clients of past purchases.
- Offer discounts for multiple purchases and regular customers.
- Provide coupons and freebies for repeat business.

Incentives are one of the easiest ways to get customers to

return to your store or restaurant. They don't cost much and they don't require any additional effort on your part. Instead, you just need to make sure that your clients know that there will be a reward for them if they come back. If you give your clients a good reason to come back, they will.

If people like you, they are likely to stick with you even if they aren't buying anything from you. So, make it easy for them to connect with you and build relationships. Offer them discounts, free shipping, or special promotions that only they will see. One of the best ways to boost your sales is to offer a reward to your existing customers. This will not only encourage your customers to come back to your business, but it will also get them excited about your business. You can also create a loyalty program and incentivize your customers to join.

Chapter 3

Understanding Your Customers' Emotions

We all know what emotions are, but some people don't know what to do with them or when to let them run their course. They see emotion as something negative, something that should be controlled or eradicated, something that will hold you back. But emotion is there for a reason.

According to neuropsychologist *David Rock*, there are two main emotional drivers in the brain that are responsible for decisions in the marketplace. These emotions are **fear and greed**. ***Fear*** motivates people to avoid something that might cause them harm or pain. ***Greed*** motivates us to pursue the things we desire. When people experience fear and greed, they are usually motivated to do what they should to avoid pain or gain pleasure.

It's there to help you navigate through life. To learn how to utilize emotions as a tool for better communication and connection, read up on the emotional intelligence framework. This is not something that comes naturally to all consumers, but it's necessary in order to build relationships that can lead to purchases. By understanding your customer's emotional state, you can guide your messaging and content to resonate with the consumer. You can then tailor your brand based on what they care about. While our emotions don't control us, they are powerful motivators. We have all had the experience of being motivated by a feeling. A friend once told me that she was never motivated to exercise until she started feeling the fear of looking at her body in the mirror.

The power of emotion comes from two sources; internal & external motivation

The power of emotion comes from two sources: *internal motivation (that is, we can make ourselves do it) and external motivation (that is, we can get others to help us).* **Internal motivation** is based on self-esteem and the belief that we are worthy. It is easier to be motivated when we believe in ourselves and our ability to do things. This is not just for people with low self-esteem. When you feel good about yourself, you are more likely to do what you know you should. In fact, your internal motivation is often stronger than your external motivation.

External motivation works through social support and encouragement from others. Sometimes it takes a little nudge to get us started.

What does this mean for you?

Well, if you are motivated by external reasons, you need to find people who will help you. If you are motivated by internal reasons, you need to have a sense of self-worth and a feeling that you are a worthwhile person. We all have these things in us, but sometimes we need to learn how to access them. I want to help you do that because the key to overcoming emotional barriers is learning to be motivated by your inner feelings rather than your external circumstances. That is why I am writing this book

Why You Should Listen to the Feeling Inside Your Customer's Head

Listening to customers' complaints is like listening to yourself. Your internal dialogue is often full of reasons why a product isn't working. It is up to you to make sure that you are always asking yourselves how your product is improving and what your customers are thinking. A lot of times, we forget that people just want to feel good and that they don't care as much about the "facts" behind their purchases as we think.

We're all familiar with the phrase *"hear no evil, see no evil."* However, this phrase is an oversimplification of how people really behave. According to the psychologist **James J. Gibson**, there are two distinct ways in which we process information: t*he analytic way (hearing), and the experiential way (feeling)*. Analytic processing occurs when we focus on words or ideas. Experiential processing occurs when we focus on the whole picture.

The feeling inside a customer's head is a powerful force. You should never ignore it. If you do, you'll lose that customer. He or she has to feel it first, and only then can you persuade them.

The only thing you really have control over in sales is your own behavior. You don't have control over your customers' behavior. You don't control the price, or the timing of your sales efforts, or the timing of your competitors' sales efforts, or any of the other factors that play into the success of your business. But what you do have control over is your own behavior. Every single day!

You can make a commitment to yourself to make the best possible effort you can toward improving your sales process, and you can make a decision to put your customer first.

You have to be the one who takes responsibility for your results, and you can't blame someone else for the way you do business. The most important thing about sales is that it's not a science.

It's not a formula. It's not an art. It's human behavior. If you want to be successful at sales, you have to behave like a human being, not like some kind of robot or a computer program. If you're going to be successful at sales, you need to be able to connect with people. I've seen a lot of salespeople who have had a hard time connecting with customers because they were too busy trying to sell. They just wanted to close the deal. They just wanted to make a sale. They were so caught up in the numbers that they forgot how to be a human being. If you want to be successful at sales, you need to start thinking like a person. You need to start thinking about what makes you human and not what makes you a machine. If you're not getting the results you want from sales, it's probably because you're being too robotic.

Understanding the Dynamics of Human Emotions

If there is one thing that has changed dramatically over the last century it is our understanding of human emotions and the impact they have on behavior. It was only 150 years ago that *Charles Darwin* and others came to understand what was then referred to as the *"unconscious mind."*

The field of neuroscience has made significant progress in understanding the brain's neural networks and how they regulate emotions, but many aspects of emotion regulation still remain a mystery.

We know that there are multiple brain regions that play a role in regulating emotions, but we do not yet fully understand which regions are responsible for which types of emotion regulation. For example, it is known that the *amygdala* plays a central role in processing fear, while the *orbitofrontal cortex (OFC)* is associated with *cognitive reappraisal*. It remains unclear whether these two brain regions work together to regulate emotional reactions.

Another issue that remains unresolved is whether the brain's emotional responses are influenced by *context*. The context can be defined broadly as the environment in which an individual is situated. In other words, the context includes the social and physical environment in which an individual is experiencing emotions. For example, if you are alone in your house and feel sad, you may not engage in any specific behavior to express sadness; however, you might cry if someone enters your home unexpectedly.

This principle is important for marketers and copywriters because it reveals why people react in certain ways to different stimuli. An emotional reaction in a visitor to a web page is the result of a trigger, which is something that causes emotions in a visitor, whether it is pleasant or unpleasant. Some triggers can be specific objects, such as images, video, or even colors. Other triggers could be actions, such as when a visitor clicks on a button or submits a form.

In psychology, the study of human emotions can be traced back to the 19th century. Emotions are a biological response of humans to stimuli, which could be internal or external.

According to psychologists, there are seven primary emotions that can be recognized by everyone: *anger, happiness, sadness, fear, disgust, surprise and contempt*. An emotion is a reaction to an event that is caused by a combination of *mental, physiological, and cognitive factors.* The goal of psychological science is to understand the nature of these emotions and how people become aware of them and express them.

For example, if you have a strong emotion like anger towards someone, you're more likely to do things that you wouldn't normally do, such as yell at that person. On the other hand, if you're having a positive emotion like happiness, you're more likely to act in a way that you wouldn't normally act. These emotional reactions are known as *emotion-based decision making*, and they affect how we process new information, how we perceive a situation, and how we respond to that situation.

Emotions can influence us in many different ways, including: how we process new information, how we perceive a situation, how we react to that situation, what we decide to do, how we make decisions.

Our emotions play a large role in how we approach any given situation. In fact, when it comes to making decisions, our emotions are what control whether we think about the problem or not, whether we consider our options, and whether we make a decision or not.

We all have different ways of dealing with these emotions. Some of us have more control over them than others. Others can't seem to control them at all. But how you deal with your emotions is important, because they can either help you or hinder you in life.

Recognizing the Differences Between Emotions and Feelings

There are three human emotions that most people are familiar with: *anger, joy, and sadness.* But there are dozens of others, and they play a big role in sales. These emotional responses include *happiness, guilt, fear, disgust, frustration, envy, admiration, anticipation, love, shame, trust, pride, and many others.* All of these emotions are present in varying degrees at any given moment. They come in response to our environment, and they influence our behavior. These emotions also affect the people around us, often triggering changes in their emotions. These reactions are called ***contagion***.

Contagion ***is one of the most powerful forces in business.***

Contagion is one of the most powerful forces in business. In fact, some experts say it's more powerful than the law of supply and demand. *Contagion* is the reason why salespeople go out to visit clients every day. It's why companies like to have lunch with prospects. It's why we call upon former colleagues or friends for referrals. And it's why we stay late at work to finish a project. Contagion can be positive or negative. It can help you sell more or it can stop you cold.

But not all contagion is created equal. Some is good. Some is bad. And some is downright evil. Why? Because while it's true that everyone is susceptible to the effects of contagion, not all contagion is created equal.

Let's take a look at some examples of good and evil contagion and see how they affect your business.

Good Contagion: As you might expect, good contagion has to do with what we're talking about here: other people. The good kind of contagion is when you are doing things that benefit others as well as yourself. For example, if you are helping someone get better or feeling better by taking care of them, this is a good contagion because you are helping them. It also helps you because it's an action that benefits someone else. But you can also have a good contagion if you are helping someone in a way that helps you feel better.

This might be something like listening to music that makes you feel better, or watching a movie that makes you feel more relaxed. Even if the music or movie is intended to make you feel good, if it helps you in any way, it is also a good contagion for you. So, here's the thing: you can help others, and it can help you, and all that you need to do is be aware of it and take advantage of it. You don't need to make a big deal out of it. You just need to be mindful.

Bad Contagion: It is when you are doing things that benefit others as well as yourself, but that also hurt someone else. For example, if you are helping someone get better or feeling better by taking care of them, this is a bad contagion because it's also hurting them. It also hurts you because it's an action that benefits someone else, and yet it also benefits you. But you can also have a bad contagion if you are helping someone in a way that hurts them.

When I am helping someone, I try to make sure that it's not hurting anyone. I always try to keep the other person's interests in mind. For example, if I am giving a friend advice on how to handle their boyfriend or girlfriend, I am only doing so if they want to hear it. If they don't want to hear it, then I won't say anything. I do the same thing with people who are going through a rough time. I try to help as much as I can without hurting anyone, even if I feel like it will hurt me.

Another example is when I am feeling down because of my own problems and I want to help someone else feel better. This is a good contagion because I am doing something that helps another person, but it also helps me. I am not just feeling down because I feel bad about myself. I am actually feeling better because I am doing something that makes me feel better. I try to make sure that this isn't hurting anyone by helping someone who needs it.

Feelings are more basic than emotions and are based on internal processes. An example of a feeling would be the sensation you get when you touch something cold.

Emotions, on the other hand, are a person's outward responses to certain situations. For instance, when you see a picture of a puppy, you might feel warm inside. An emotion, however, could be feeling happy, sad, or angry.

There are three types of feelings: *Negative Feelings, Positive Feelings, Neutral Feelings.* A feeling is classified as either negative or positive depending on its effect on a person's mood.

Negative feelings tend to make people unhappy. For example, if you feel sad, then you may be feeling a negative feeling.

Positive feelings, on the other hand, generally make people happy. For example, if you feel good about something, you may be feeling a positive feeling.

Neutral feelings are neither positive nor negative. For example, if you feel indifferent, you are experiencing a neutral feeling. The first step in feeling more positive is to understand what causes negative feelings and how they can be avoided. Then, we can use this understanding to learn to identify when we feel a negative emotion. We can also use it to recognize when we feel a positive feeling.

Finally, we can use this knowledge to determine what we can do to improve our moods.

How to Interpret Your Customer's Feelings

In short, the key takeaway from the study is that emotions are hard to quantify, and even more difficult to interpret. When customers don't react to a message the same way that you intended, don't jump to conclusions. Rather, it could be because the message wasn't delivered in a way that resonates with the individual. To understand a customer's feelings, first identify their emotional state. Then, ask yourself*: Is it constructive? Is it negative?*

Negative emotions, such as anger, can be quite useful in getting the attention of a busy, distracted customer. So, too, are positive emotions such as joy.

By identifying your customer's emotional state, you can determine how to react appropriately. If you're frustrated or angry at a customer, for example, you might want to change your tone. If you're a patient person, you might try to make them feel better by offering a solution to the problem they're having. If you see a customer who seems sad, you might try to cheer them up by making them laugh.

If you notice someone who looks bored, you might change your strategy so that they're excited about whatever it is you're talking about. Once you know what your customer's emotional state is, it becomes easy to understand why he or she wants to buy from you.

If you want to interpret your customer's feelings, the first thing to do is to learn what their emotions are. There are five major emotions: *happy, sad, angry, fearful, and confused*. These are the main emotions that you will find in your customers.

Happy: Happy customers are enthusiastic and excited about what you have to offer. They feel motivated and confident when they are talking with you. Happy customers are very interested in your products and services.

Sad: Sad customers are disappointed and unhappy with you. They may have problems with your products and services. Sad customers don't seem motivated to do business with you.

Angry: Angry customers feel irritated when they are

talking with you. They will be annoyed and impatient with you. If you are not careful, you might get an angry customer because they don't understand what you're saying.

Fearful: Fearful customers are worried about your products or services. They are afraid of losing money if they buy from you. Customers who feel afraid are less likely to buy from you.

Confused: Confused customers may feel confused and frustrated when they talk to you. They are not sure if they want to purchase your products or not.

As you can see, you need to be observant to determine whether your customers are happy, sad, angry, fearful, or confused.

Most companies are built around the concept of understanding and serving the customer. To do so, they need to be able to interpret and reflect on what their customers want. By observing and interpreting their emotions, customers can tell companies what they need. By using empathy, companies can relate to their customers and understand what drives them. This is the foundation of great customer service.

Empathy is an essential skill for a company to build relationships with their customers. It’s the ability to understand a customer’s needs and feelings, which helps companies serve their customers better.

Chapter 4

Rules to Creating Great Product and How to Keep Customers

To write an effective product description, you need to understand what your ideal customer wants and needs. You also have to be able to identify the differences between your competitors' products. And finally, you need to know how to use those differences to your advantage.

A lot of times, the reason a customer buys a product is because of their experience with a company or brand. The fact is that, with the internet, most people are looking for ways to save time and money.

The key to successful product development is to always remember that the product doesn't exist until the marketer has the data to support its existence.

In other words, your product can't be created unless it's possible for people to understand what it is, why they need it, and how it will benefit them.

If there is anything we've learned about businesses, it's that you must make a conscious decision to treat every customer like gold. They're business's greatest asset and the company can't afford to be indifferent to them. The key to creating great products is to take something people really want, and create it.

The trick is not to just copy what other successful businesses are doing. Instead, you should look for ideas that nobody else is offering. There are only so many ways to design a guitar for instance. Look for ideas that other guitarists are missing. You can create a new genre by combining elements of two existing genres. Or, if you find yourself having trouble with a particular guitar model, look to see what other guitarists are doing with similar guitars.

The good news is that there are some rules you can follow to help make the customer experience with you better. Some of these rules include:

- Have high-quality product.
- Provide real value.
- Offer customer service.
- Make sure your website is optimized for mobile.
- And of course, create a strong brand identity.

Below are a few key rules for creating products worth keeping:

- **Think like your customers:** Before starting to design a new product, take some time to think about how the experience could be improved. Do you already have an existing product that's not perfect? Is there a pain point in your life that your customers are dealing with right now? Think about how you might help solve those problems.
- **Think about what people do with your products:** Ask yourself; what are the things I really like to do? What's the next thing I'm likely to need? What would I buy if I could afford to?
- **Do your research:** There's no such thing as a *"perfect"* product; even something you've been working on for months won't be perfect. But if you know your competitors' products inside and out, you can understand what they're doing wrong. You may find that you have ideas that complement theirs, and you can use them to improve your own product.

If you have a good idea for a new product or service, how do you go about developing it?

The process is not as simple as you might think. It's an

iterative process, and it takes time. You will need to gather feedback from your customers to see what works and what doesn't. You will need to test and experiment to refine and perfect your product or service. You may need to try things out in the real world to see how people respond. This is where a business plan comes in.

A business plan is a written document that provides you with details about your idea. It will help you to decide whether to pursue your idea or not. A business plan can help you get funding, develop a market, and build a business. It will help you get the money you need to grow your business.

It is a roadmap for your venture, which can be a daunting task. It is a plan of action that shows you have thought through all aspects of your idea before you begin. A business plan is also a useful tool for anyone who is trying to start a business.

Creating an Efficient Service Model

One of the biggest mistakes I see when creating services is the failure to create a clear service model from the start. And that means you don't get to experience the satisfaction of delivering what your customers actually need. For example, there are many companies that have created a product that can be delivered via an on-demand service (think Uber). But the real value isn't the product itself. The real value is in the customer relationship and the knowledge that comes from being able to provide them with a better product at a lower cost. I'm not saying you can't build a service company without having a product. You can. But it takes a little more work.

You have to figure out what your product is first, and then build a service around it. I was reminded of this recently when I had the chance to sit down with a senior executive at a well known tech company. He had built a great team and they were really doing something awesome. They had built an app that could do something really useful. They also had a strong product/market fit. What was missing? They didn't have a service model. They didn't really have a service in mind. They were building their service by creating a product.

This is a mistake. I know a lot of people think they are doing it, but in reality, what you are building is a product with a service attached to it. I'm not talking about the service model of the business, or even the technical service model of your application. I'm talking about the service model of your product. If you don't understand the difference between a product and a service, you might be building a product with a service attached to it.

The reason I say this is because I've seen a number of services built by startups that do not have a clear service model. In many cases, I think they are building a product with a service attached to it. The problem is that they don't realize it. So, let's take a look at some examples.

Product vs Service

I've seen a lot of people in the past say "You know what, I'm going to build a service. I can get more customers this way." Or, "I'm going to build a service, because it will be a lot easier to monetize."

These statements are often made by a business or startup that has never built a service before, and does not understand the difference between a product and a service. This is why you need to understand the difference between a product and a service before you decide to build one. The reason I say that a service has a clear service model is that it is based on something that is repeatable. Think about it for a second.

A service is something that you offer to other people. You're not offering the service to yourself. You're offering the service to someone else. If you build a service, your target market is other people. That's the core difference between a product and a service. If you build a product, your target market is yourself. You're offering the product to yourself. If you're building a product, then you need to have a clear product vision.

You need to have an idea of what the product is and who it's for. That's going to give you a lot more clarity than just saying *"I want to build this app."* But if you're offering a service, you're not selling anything to yourself. You're offering a service to other people. You can offer a service without building a product. You don't need to build a product before you offer a service. If you offer a service, your target market is other people.

So you don't need to be so focused on your product vision. You need to have a much clearer picture of who the people are that you're serving.

Here's the key to creating a high-profit service business without the headaches: create a model that allows you to profitably scale your services from zero to one million dollars per year without having to do anything except put out better value than your competition.

There are two key differences between the business model of a service and a product. First, a service must deliver value over time. Second, a service requires repeat visits.

The first of these means that a service needs to have an ongoing relationship with its customers. The second means that it should have a clear plan for making sure customers keep coming back. While the customer may be able to use a product in one way or another, the best services must be used over time and should build a relationship with the customer.

If you're an individual service provider, then it may be more efficient to run a business model with fewer employees. If you're running a company that provides a lot of different services, like a restaurant, you may need to make sure that your staff can handle all the work, rather than trying to serve fewer customers at the same time.

There are four primary ways a business can structure itself to operate efficiently. They are: *horizontal integration, vertical integration, decentralized coordination, and disjointed management.*

Horizontal integration means integrating multiple business units in order to cut costs and reduce redundancy, allowing a company to offer the same service to more customers at a lower cost than if they were to use their separate units.

Vertical integration means integrating the supply chain, selling the products themselves, and using internal expertise for manufacturing, warehousing, and distribution to save costs.

Decentralized coordination is an efficient model when a company works with a partner who provides a specialized skill set.

Lastly, **Disjointed management** refers to companies that work separately without a cohesive strategy.
An effective service model should be based on a few core principles. It should offer something unique, be affordable,

have high value, be tailored to your audience, and have an easy return policy. A well-constructed service model will attract customers and drive conversions. It can be a huge part of your success if it's designed with the right mindset.

Improving Your Relationship Management Skills and Building a Customer Advisory Board

When I spoke with a friend in a marketing company that specialized in social media, the VP of client relations said he didn't like to talk to people. I was surprised. As CEO, he had a lot of employees. So he created an employee advisory board to help make decisions. Then he took it further; He created a relationship management software system for his company, which helps employees track customers and their interactions with the company. The goal is to build loyalty and improve the quality of the relationship. To be a successful relationship manager, you need to know how to manage relationships.

The key to managing relationships successfully is to focus on one thing at a time. Do too many things at once and you risk creating chaos for yourself and your customers. Also, you should take your customer's time into consideration, as they are your most important asset. When you're building relationships with your customers, you want to focus on what you can offer them that they don't already have. So instead of trying to be everything to everyone, be just enough for your ideal customer—and then give that customer something extra.

Relationship marketing is a new concept for many businesses, *but it's not new to the world of marketing*. In fact, I think it's one of the most effective ways to market a business today. As an example, let's say you own a company that sells furniture. You might think about how you can promote your business. You could advertise in local newspapers or on TV, but you know that these methods will not attract your ideal customer. Instead, you should focus on establishing relationships with your customers by using relationship marketing.

How would you go about finding your ideal customer?

First, think about your target audience. Who are your ideal customers? What do they need? What do they want? How can you help them meet their needs and desires? This is the first step in establishing a relationship with your ideal customer.

Second, *Think about your product;* Do you offer a product that your customers need? If so, what problem does it solve? Are your customers willing to pay for your product? If so, why are they willing to pay?

Third; *Decide on Your Pricing Structure;* When deciding on the pricing structure for your product, it's important to consider your ideal customer. What kind of person will be most likely to buy your product? What is their buying process? How much do they make? How much are they willing to spend on your product? If your ideal customer is someone who makes $50,000 a year, then you should price your product at $30 a month.

If your ideal customer is someone who makes $15,000 a year, then you should price your product at $20 a month. The more your product is worth to the average person, the lower the price should be. To calculate your initial pricing, start by determining how much money your customers are currently spending on similar products. For example, if you're selling software, find out what your customers pay for similar products and multiply that number by your price. If your ideal customer makes $50,000 a year, you should price your product at $50 a month.

Once you have an idea of what you want to sell, you need to decide where you will sell it. Do you want to sell online, on a site like **Etsy** or **Amazon**, or through a local store or market place? Each of these positions has advantages and disadvantages, but you'll have to consider all of them to make a good decision.

If you want to make more money and achieve more of your goals, there's no doubt about it: You'll need help. To get that help, you'll need a **customer advisory board (CAB)**. A **CAB** is a group of people who provide advice, guidance, and counsel based on their experience with and knowledge of your business. They will work with you to help you get ahead. But it doesn't end there. There are two types of **CAB**: **advisory and executive.**

The ***advisory CAB*** gives you the information you need to make your business better, while the ***executive CAB*** provides you with guidance and leadership. Both are essential to your success.

Here are nine reasons why a **CAB** can help you achieve more in business.

They can keep you on track: In order for your business to grow, you'll need to stay on track. The **CAB** can be an invaluable tool because they'll keep you on track with your vision and help you stay focused on what you want to achieve. They'll also help you avoid distractions that might get in your way of reaching your goals.

They'll bring everyone together: You're going to need to collaborate with other members of your CAB when it comes to setting goals and working towards them. Having a CAB meeting will allow you to share ideas, and then take action on them together.

They can help you stay on budget: While budgets are important, they can also be tricky to work with. A CAB can help you stay on budget by having everyone involved come up with ideas that make sense for your budget, and then sharing these ideas so everyone is aware of them.

They can keep you on schedule: One of the biggest

problems with having a business is that you have to juggle everything at once. Your customers, your employees, and your marketing efforts all have their own priorities. A CAB can keep you on schedule by helping you set deadlines for each of those things.

They'll keep you accountable: The last thing you want is someone who's important to you not keeping you accountable. If you have a CAB, they'll be the ones you're accountable to.

They can help you get feedback from your team: Having a CAB can help you get feedback from your team. You may have certain members of your team who are more experienced than others, and you can work with them to find out what they think about your business and how they feel it could be improved.

They can help you decide where to focus your time: A CAB can help you decide where to focus your time. This means you can focus on what really matters to your business, and you can delegate other things to other people in your company.

They can help you decide what to do next: A CAB can help you decide what to do next. For example, if you're not getting the results you need from your marketing efforts, then you can use a CAB to help you decide which strategies you should try.

They can help you make smart decisions: A CAB can help you make smart decisions. This means you can make more informed decisions when it comes to your business, and you can take action based on those decisions.

A successful business model revolves around the quality of the relationships you build and maintain. When you start a business, you usually have a lot of friends, acquaintances, and contacts. Your relationship management skills are key to your success.

If you want to make money and not lose money, you need to start building relationships.

The good news is that you can learn how to do this in just a few weeks. The first thing you need to do is to stop doing what you're doing right now. This means that you need to stop spending your time on your existing network. When you spend your time with people who are negative, toxic, or otherwise unhelpful, they will affect your business. They will drag you down, and they will keep you from reaching your goals.

The next step is to start building relationships with people who are positive, productive, and helpful. You can find these people by networking, attending events, or participating in forums. If you're interested in joining a community of like-minded individuals who share your interests, you can also join online communities. If you're looking to become an entrepreneur, it's important that you don't just learn how to manage your own personal relationships.

You also need to learn about the relationships of others. Once you've started learning about the relationships of others, you should begin to focus on the relationships that you have. By focusing on the relationships you already have, you will be able to work on improving them. When you build a network of positive relationships, you can start making progress in your business.

As you're building your network, you may encounter challenges. This is completely normal, and there are ways to overcome these challenges. The more you practice networking, the better you will become at it.

Be aware of what you're doing; If you're trying to grow a business, you need to be aware of what you're doing. You need to stay on top of your business and make sure that you are on top of all of the things that you need to do. If you don't stay on top of your business, you could find yourself losing out on a lot of money.

Chapter 5

Importance of Maintaining an Ethical Environment in the Workplace

We all have to work to earn a living. That means we have to be responsible and follow the rules. We also have to make sure that our workplace is safe. All these things must be maintained in the workplace. The company's reputation and its safety record depend on how well we do. If we don't maintain a proper environment, we are bound to have problems.

We need to be careful about how we talk to others, especially our customers. There may be a reason why someone does what he or she does. It doesn't mean that we have to agree with them. But, we need to be careful not to hurt their feelings. Our job is to do a good job, and to provide what we promise. If we are good to our customers, they will return for more. We can also get fired if we don't maintain a proper environment.

So, we must be careful and do what we say we are going to do. When we take time off for our own personal reasons, it is only fair that we take time off from work as well.

We must also be careful when dealing with our coworkers. We shouldn't gossip about them or bad-mouth them. When we say things about our coworkers, we must be careful because it might reflect badly on us. For example, if you say something about your boss, you might get demoted. And, if you say something about your coworkers, you might get them demoted. In some cases, you could even get fired.

It's easy to get caught up in the day-to-day responsibilities that come along with your career. While the work you're doing may seem important, it isn't always easy to see just how important you are to others and to your company.

You're responsible for creating a healthy environment for everyone working under you, but it's easy to get bogged down in the daily grind. The way you treat your employees will have a huge impact on the kind of workplace they feel comfortable working in. Being respectful, treating them with dignity, and being a positive role model will go a long way in creating a positive and productive workplace.

Ethical standards are important in any business setting. They are particularly important when dealing with consumers and clients. If a company is seen as unethical, it can lose its customers, employees, and ultimately, its business.

There are some very basic ethical guidelines that every business should follow. These include, but aren't limited to: *protecting the privacy of customer information, keeping promises to customers, not accepting illegal products or services, and treating everyone fairly.*

One of the many reasons why ethical environments are important for the workplace is because they allow employees to thrive while working for an organization. An ethical culture promotes trust in others, which fosters higher morale and productivity.

With the growing demand for technology professionals to enter the workforce and to succeed in this high demand industry, many people are often taken advantage of by unethical employers and supervisors. The workplace should always be a place of trust and respect.

Helping Your Employees Overcome Feelings of Anxiety and Low Self-esteem in the Business Space

One of the hardest things to overcome in the workplace is anxiety and low self-esteem. Anxiety and low self-esteem can cause many problems for businesses such as high turnover, poor communication, and lack of productivity. Luckily, there are some simple ways to help your employees overcome this in the workplace. For example, *consider having team-building exercises every month.* These can include ice breakers, lunchtime games, and activities that bring people together.

The next step in helping your employees overcome feelings of anxiety and low self-esteem is to create a culture where they feel comfortable being themselves. To do this, you must be willing to listen to them when they express their opinions and feelings. This will ensure that you don't get caught up in what they say, but rather in how they say it. If you can't handle that, then you might want to look into hiring a life coach to help guide you through the process.

Another way is to set goals that require employees to do things that they may feel that they can't accomplish. These exercises will help them to overcome feelings of low self-esteem and develop new skills that they didn't know they had.

As I mentioned earlier, the most difficult obstacle is the ability to separate your personal life from the professional one. The only way to succeed in the corporate world is to stay focused on the job. If you can successfully keep your personal life separate from your professional life, then you'll be able to successfully manage the stress of working in a big company.

The main reason why people choose to work in the business space over a non-profit is that they believe that making a profit will help them reach their personal goals faster. People who work in the business space are more likely to feel that they need to earn money in order to get ahead than people who work in the nonprofit space. So, if you are in charge of developing the career and growth plans for your company's employees, then you need to help them understand why they're working in the business space.

Establishing a Reliable Reputation and Track Record

A reputation is something that's earned over time. When we build a reputation for reliability, we're building a track record. Think about someone who gets into a car accident or has a flat tire. The car dealer isn't always going to be the last one they call for help, because they need to repair the damage and fix whatever problems the car might have. The mechanic isn't going to be the first one they call because he or she hasn't yet established a reputation for being reliable. This is the same logic that applies to businesses, too.

A lot of entrepreneurs think that word of mouth is the only thing that matters when it comes to reputation. Unfortunately, that's not the case. There are plenty of people who can help establish a great reputation for your business, and a great reputation can be just as powerful as word of mouth in terms of helping you grow your business. You can't rely on other people to do the marketing for you, but there are lots of things you can do to help build and maintain a reliable reputation and track record for your business.

People can talk about your product or service on the internet, either positively or negatively, but there's really no way to determine whether or not this is going to be accurate. You can't control what they're going to say, but you can control what you do. *Do what you say you're going to do. Be honest. Tell the truth. Be a good listener. Be a good communicator. Be helpful and polite. Give and take.*

These are the qualities that will help your customers trust you and give you the opportunity to establish yourself as a reliable and trustworthy person in the industry.

Providing Realistic Expectations

Expectations are set by the buyer and seller at the moment the deal is made. When you're looking to buy or sell something, your expectations are often set by what you see. But there are a lot of variables that come into play between the time you make your search and the moment the transaction occurs.

You'll need to communicate to your potential buyers why

they should expect what they do, and how their expectations should change.

While it's true that the longer customers wait, the more likely it is that they'll forget about your business or give up completely, they're also far more likely to spend money if they feel that they don't have much of a choice. If you offer a free trial, make sure that you include clear guidelines around when that free trial ends. And if you have limited quantity available, say, for example, only 20 units of your product for sale, make sure that you clearly communicate to customers when that limit has been reached.

When people feel like they know what's expected of them, they feel more empowered to perform their tasks. When they don't feel prepared for something, however, they tend to lose motivation. One of the best option is to ensure that a customer feels empowered to do their part to clearly communicate expectations. And to make sure you're conveying what you want the customer to expect, use the word *"should"* sparingly. Instead, describe your expectation in terms of a *"must," or "ought."* This will help ensure the customer is on the same page with you.

Offering a Value-Based Commitment

You've heard of the sales term *"commitment"* before. But in order for you to truly commit to something, there has to be some kind of perceived value for the thing being offered. *So what is the perceived value of the commitment?* In my experience, you have to make a promise that is very close to what you want to happen. For example, if you're planning a trip, the promise has to be for a trip where you're going to do something fun or worthwhile. If it's not close to that, you're not going to really commit to it. This is especially true for the first time. You're not really committing to a trip to Hawaii if you only promised to go somewhere else.

You can tell people to commit to something, but you can't force them to do it. So what you want to do is give them a reason to commit to it.

Commitments come in two forms: ***explicit and implicit***.

Explicit commitments are what you can actually see. They include items such as: *I'm going to eat my vegetables every day, I'm going to save money, I'm going to lose weight, I'm going to be loyal to you, etc.*

Implicit commitments, on the other hand, are based on how people act. These are things like; You make me feel safe, You make me proud, You give me hope, You show me that I matter, etc.

The value in both forms of commitment comes from what you can offer the consumer.

Chapter 6

Applying Emotional Intelligence to Marketing Strategies

There are different ways to market products or services. Some companies use traditional marketing strategies such as billboards, TV ads, radio commercials, and newspaper advertisements. These strategies can be very effective, but they are only used for short periods of time. They don't last very long because people will forget about the advertising message after a few minutes.

Another way to promote products or services is through social media. Social media websites such as **Facebook, Instagram, TikTok, LinkedIn, Twitter, YouTube, and Google+** are very popular among marketers. Social media allows marketers to connect with their customers. Customers can share information about products and services they have purchased or like. They can also interact with one another.

They can also use a website such as **Pinterest** to advertise their products or services.

A lack of emotional intelligence can cause people to make mistakes when marketing. Consumers may feel like they have to buy something because someone they admire did. Or they'll feel pressured by other people who are more knowledgeable than they are to buy a particular item. They don't need to feel this pressure or that fear. All they need is to know what they want and why. Once they know, they'll feel confident in their choice.

Most companies aren't very good at applying emotional intelligence to marketing strategies. There are two parts of emotional intelligence: ***empathy and intuition.***

When you're empathetic, you can see yourself in someone else. This means that if you can truly understand your customers and their needs, you can create products and services that will actually help them. And when you have a lot of insight into your customers' needs, you'll be better equipped to know what your customers need to hear and what they need to avoid.

In the same way, your marketing strategy may seem exciting or cool in your head, but if your prospects and customers aren't buying your products or services because they see a problem that needs to be solved, then excitement isn't going to work. To make a real difference, you need to use emotional intelligence to help guide your decisions about how to communicate with potential customers and employees.

How to Use Emotions to Increase Sales and Retention

In today's world, emotions are an important aspect of business. They can help you to increase your sales, and they can make you successful in your company. For example, if you are worried about losing your job, you might have trouble concentrating. That means you would not be able to do your work well. If you're happy and motivated, however, you can concentrate better and perform at a high level. You can use emotions in different ways. The way you feel can affect your productivity. It's important to choose your emotions carefully. You should do things that you enjoy and that you are confident in.

When you enjoy doing your work and you feel confident about your work, you will have a better chance of succeeding in your business.

Many studies suggest that humans are wired to respond to positive emotions more intensely than negative ones. This makes emotional appeals very powerful tools to increase sales and retention. A few common examples of this include using humor to encourage customers to buy more, or using fear to build trust. But when it comes to the business world, negative emotions can be even more effective in achieving a goal. For example, fear is one of the strongest motivators for people to take action. This makes negative emotions like anger and disappointment an essential part of any marketing strategy. While negative emotions are often ignored, they can actually be used to create powerful brand messages.

Here's why:

- Negative emotions are strong motivators.
- Emotions are powerful motivators.
- People respond more strongly to negative emotions

than positive ones.

When you want to influence someone emotionally, make sure that the emotion you are trying to evoke is something they are feeling. If you want to influence someone with a positive emotion, then choose something like happiness, love or optimism. But if you want to influence someone with a negative emotion, use anger, sadness or fear. There are many other types of emotions that are powerful and motivating, including excitement, joy, surprise, frustration, hate, pride, and disgust.

However, there are certain emotions that are more effective at influencing people than others. Here are three of the strongest:

Anger: The emotion of anger is a strong one. It is also the most powerful emotion to influence people with. When people feel angry, they have a strong desire to do something about it. The power of this emotion comes from two sources. First, the fact that it is a natural human emotion means that it is an easy emotion to get people to feel. Second, it is a very strong emotion. Anger can be very powerful because it is so strong. For this reason, it is a good emotion to use when you want to influence people.

Fear: Another emotion that is important is fear. Fear is the emotion that we feel when we are afraid of something bad happening to us or to others. Fear is one of the strongest emotions because it is a natural human emotion. In addition, fear is also a very strong emotion.

Sadness: The last emotion that we will look at is sadness. Sadness is an emotion that we feel when we are sad. People often feel sadness when they have lost something or someone that they love. Sadness is a very powerful emotion because it is such a natural human emotion.

You've seen a lot of data showing that emotional customers are loyal customers. But you've also seen a lot of data showing that emotional customers don't buy as much as rational customers.

So if emotions matter, why aren't marketers working to make their products and services emotional? Why aren't they using emotion to increase sales and retention?

The reason is that emotions are difficult to control. In other words, it's difficult for us to create a feeling we want in our customers. This makes emotional appeals hard to use.

Most marketers don't have a good understanding of the science behind emotions, so they don't know how to use them to increase sales and retention. But this doesn't mean emotional marketing isn't effective. In fact, *the best way to use emotional appeals is to understand them. And the best way to understand emotions is through the study of human emotion.*

What is Emotional Marketing?

Emotional marketing is any form of marketing that uses emotions to sell. It can be anything from a simple email to a full-fledged advertising campaign. To be clear, when we talk about emotional marketing, we're not talking about marketing using emotions to manipulate customers. That's called *emotional manipulation.* Instead, *we're talking about using emotions in a positive way to get customers to buy more or use your product. This includes using humor, fear, anger, shame, and gratitude.*

When we are in a positive state, we are more likely to be kind to others and want to help them. We tend to trust people in a positive emotional state, and it makes us more willing to be vulnerable with those who are close to us. The negative emotional button makes us feel afraid and angry when someone is threatening us. We may be less trusting of those who are trying to hurt us.

Why Use Emotions?

One reason to use emotions is because it's a proven method for increasing sales and retention. Emotional triggers have been used since the beginning of marketing history to persuade people to buy. We've all seen the **"Buy now"** button on **Amazon**, the emotional pull that convinces people to make an immediate purchase. If we want to increase sales, we need to be able to create similar emotional pull for our products. There's nothing better than when you see a product that makes you feel something.

Chapter 7

Developing a Winning Culture in Business

A key element of building any culture, especially one that's focused on results, is to understand and appreciate the fact that there's a difference between a company and its people. People matter. At least, they matter if you want to succeed. People who are engaged with what's happening around them, tend to be happier and more productive. They are also more likely to enjoy working with their co-workers.

So; if you want to be able to create a winning culture in your business, you must make sure that you engage everyone around you. Your employees are the ones who will ultimately help you build your business, and drive its success.

A strong culture is often defined as a set of values, traditions, and practices shared by an organization or team.

The key to creating a winning culture in business is to start with your employees. Your company may already have a strong culture in place. If it does, great. If it doesn't, consider whether the culture you have is consistent with the vision you have for your company. However, a winning culture in business is something everyone talks about in terms of what's good for business and good for the bottom line.

How many times have you sat through a meeting where the discussion revolved around the lack of urgency? Maybe you've attended too many meetings where you left wondering why you even bothered showing up in the first place. If you're looking for a culture of urgency in your business, it's easier than you might think. Start by being open about your company's culture.

A business culture that is focused on serving customers and satisfying employees is a vital part of any company. Cultures that focus on growth, success, and building a strong, long-term foundation for the business are the ones that thrive and the ones that will see consistent success. In short, a winning culture exists when everyone is working together and on the same page.

Here are elements to creating and fostering a winning culture: *a shared vision, trust, clarity of purpose, accountability, and respect.*

One of the keys to developing a winning culture is setting clear and specific values. The first step is to decide what your values are, and to establish the tone and level of commitment to those values throughout the company.

Second, you need to create an organizational structure that reflects the values of the company. Finally, the company needs a clear vision for how the organization is going to operate.

When a company adopts values that reflect the mission and vision, the employees feel proud to be a part of it and perform at a higher level.

How to Encourage Customers to Refer

According to research, 68% of consumers said that they would refer a friend or family member who purchased something from a business they like. But only 16% of those customers actually referred someone, which means the rest of us are missing out on a huge opportunity to build customer referrals. So; how can you encourage your customers to become advocates for your brand? There are a few key tactics to keep in mind.

There are two main reasons why you should encourage customers to refer you: First, because it's the ethical thing to do and second, because word-of-mouth advertising is one of the most effective means of growing a business.

Once your referral program is set up, you need to focus on providing rewards and incentives that make it worth people's while to refer you. People will always need a reason to do something, so give them a good one. For example, you could provide your referral program partners with free product or discounts in return for referring their friends. You can also send personalized *"thank-you"* messages to people who refer you and provide a little incentive to keep them interested.

Another great way to encourage referrals is by giving your customers an easy way to share their experiences with other people online. For example, you could create an online forum or blog where customers can post reviews, ratings and photos of their experience with you and others can read about their experiences. This type of sharing provides more visibility for your business, and it's a great way to build trust and loyalty with your customers. You can also ask your customers to become brand ambassadors by encouraging them to spread the word about your business on their social networks and blogs. Just make sure that you don't pressure them into doing this, as it might turn them off. Ask them what they would like to share and make it easy for them to do so.

The key here is to make it fun. When people share their experiences, they often enjoy it so much that they want to do it again, so it's important to make sure they don't feel pressured into it. The bottom line is that it's good business to encourage referrals, and it's good customer service to reward them when people do. Your customers will appreciate it and you'll reap the rewards of growing a loyal, referral-based business.

Conclusion

This skill, called *emotional intelligence,* is a huge determinant of success and happiness in business, social life, and general personal life. I'm sure learning how to use the new science of Emotional Intelligence to increase customer loyalty and retention is an aspect you're extremely knoledgeable on.

In addition to all that has been recommended in this book, you have to understand the feelings of your customers. Otherwise, you won't be able to provide them with the type of service that they need.

Customers are always concerned about their satisfaction. If they feel that they are getting the service that they want, they will tell others about it and recommend your business to others. If you want to be successful in the business world, you need to know how to deal with people. You must always be sensitive to people's feelings and be polite. You must listen carefully to what they are saying.

You have to remember that everyone has different needs and wants. So, your job is to satisfy those needs. This is how you will increase customer loyalty. If you are polite, you will be a pleasant person. You will be liked and you will be successful.

SPECIAL BONUS!

Want These 2 Bonus EBooks For Free?

Get FREE, Unlimited Access To These and All of Our New Books By Joining Our Community

CLICK HERE TO JOIN

Thank You!

Thank you for taking the time to check out my work - I hope you enjoy reading it as much as I enjoyed writing it! Authors wouldn't be anywhere without readers like you, so your support **REALLY** means a lot. I'm a firm believer that books don't need to be expensive or difficult to get hold of - so I want to encourage **EVERYONE** to enjoy the pleasure of books - and not just mine.

I would be grateful if you could **WRITE ME A REVIEW** on the product detail page about how this book has helped you. Your review means a lot to me, as I would love to hear about your successes.

Nothing makes me happier than knowing that my work has aided someone in achieving their goals and progressing in life; which would likewise motivate me to improve and serve you better, and also encourage other readers to get influenced positively by my work.

Your feedback means so much to me, and I will never take it for granted.

I'd love to hear from you if you have any recommendations

of your own, so please do get in touch if you've read anything awesome lately.

If you ever have any questions, you can get in touch at sam@samamoo.com.

I want you to enjoy your reading experience; your satisfaction is my number one priority. You are well appreciated for reading this book.

Thank you, have a wonderful day!

About The Author

Sam Amoo is a writer and publisher focused on business growth, habits, decision making, and continuous improvement. He is the author of Sell Like Titans.

He teaches business owners on how to grow and run business at the same time, without getting stuck between the two worlds of growing and running business. He helps entrepreneurs build their dreams, by combining c*oncepts, ideas, and insights to make problem-solving easy.*

He has trained over four hundred successful business owners, and mentored over a hundred entrepreneurs excelling in digital and online business. Everything he does is fueled by his love for entrepreneurship, wealth development, diversity, and advancement.

Connect with us here:

Instagram: https://instagram.com/_amoosam

Facebook: https://fb.me/samamoo.official

Twitter: https://twitter.com/samamooofficial

LinkedIn: https://www.linkedin.com/company/samamoo

Email: sam@samamoo.com

Other Book

- Sell Like Titans
- Time Management For Busy People

Made in the USA
Monee, IL
04 November 2026

67379298R00085